Spiritual Awakening Journal

Spiritual Awakening Journal

Daily Reflections to Attract Positivity and
Reconnect with Your Truest Self

CASSANDRA BODZAK

**ROCKRIDGE
PRESS**

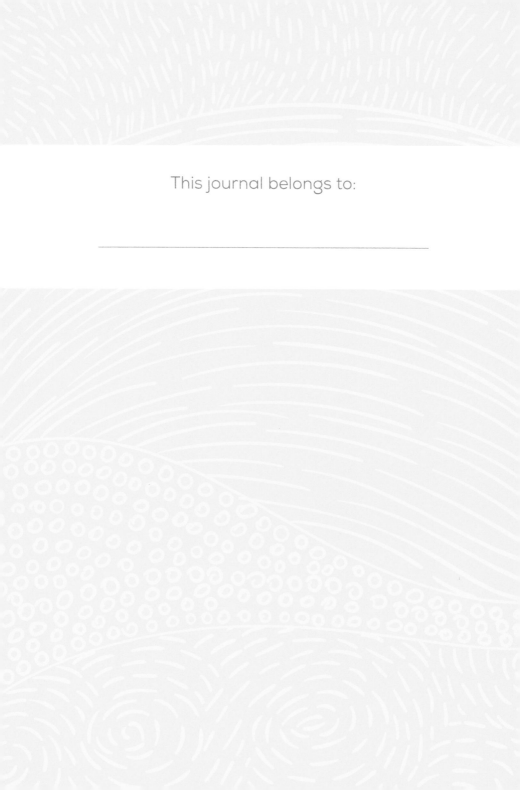

This journal belongs to:

_____

Introduction

Welcome to your _Spiritual Awakening Journal,_ a place where you can come each day for reflection, expansion, and guidance along your path to greater spiritual connection. Each spiritual awakening journey is unique; however, the exercises in this book will hold space for the kind of deeper inquiry that assists all spiritual awakening paths.

What exactly is spiritual awakening, anyway? An important question to begin with! Spiritual awakening is about growth: a process of coming home to our true divine nature—one that is whole, authentic, and our best self. It's about honoring that we are more than our bodies and part of something far greater. We start opening up to new states of awareness and truths from deep in our soul. We begin looking at our world through different eyes. It's about developing a personal relationship to the divine (or higher power or powers by whatever name or form you prefer)—whether it's internal or external, tangible or intangible, visible or invisible—and tapping into its intuitive, ever-flowing guidance. As we do, we realize benefits, such as experiencing more awareness in our daily life; reconnecting with what matters; feeling more empowered, optimistic, and positive; and—my personal favorite—living life with a sense of wonder and reverence. It can even seem magical.

Often, a spiritual awakening begins with a bang. Mine certainly did: My brother received a devastating health diagnosis, and my world shattered instantly. Little did I know this is a common place for an awakening journey to begin. That moment looks different for everyone. For some, it's a job loss, health scare, divorce, or breakup. For others, it can be losing a loved one. It can also come from overwhelming feelings, perhaps of being stuck or wanting more out of life. Wherever you are, trust that this book found you because it's time for this journey.

So what makes me the perfect guide for this trek up the spiritual mountain? Well, I've been guiding people of all different ages, in countries around the world, on their spiritual awakening journey for over a decade. I've worked with clients one-on-one and in my group program as well as in countless workshops and retreats and through my other books. Even though no two spiritual paths are alike, I know my way around this mountain, and I'm excited to help make your unique spiritual journey a pleasurable one.

Here, you will find journal prompts, affirmations, and practices, all designed to assist you on this wondrous journey. The prompts seek to inspire you to think in different ways, contemplate new spiritual concepts, and dig down to unearth deeper truths. Don't worry about getting it right—all that matters is that you answer each question as honestly as possible. This isn't a test; it's an exploration! The affirmations are there for you to take with you into your day to contemplate these new concepts and spiritual truths. You don't have to fully assimilate everything at once. Instead, think of it like eating: You'll chew on it, and eventually it will digest. Finally, the practices are here to help you integrate and embody your awakening. You'll engage in various activities that will bring you beyond contemplation to the experience of a spiritual truth.

I encourage you to trust the process and yourself. You will find exercises that work better for you than others, and that's okay. As a result of showing up consistently, your spiritual awakening journey will transform you. You won't be able to look at your life the same way or show up to your life the same, and you'll be so much happier for it!

Here's an affirmation to get you started on your way:

> I happily show up each day for my spiritual awakening adventure. I trust that it's unfolding for my greatest good.

Visioning

Imagine you had a wand that you could wave over your life to completely transform any and all areas. What would you use it for? How would your life look when your magical makeover was complete?

Possibilities

Do you remember a time in your childhood when you felt like anything was possible? Reflect on one or more memories of your early years, when you felt the infinite possibilities available, and write about them on the following lines.

Self-Expression

Our world likes to put us in a neat, easily labeled box, yet our spirits are so multidimensional, we never truly fit. What different facets of you seek to spill over? How can you embrace them more in your life?

Animal Essence

If you had to choose an animal that reflects your personality, which animal would you choose and why? Pick a second animal that reflects the energy you want to embody more of. What are the characteristics of these two animals?

Self-Discovery

Write a story (or stories) from your life that you feel represents the true essence of who you are. What do you feel like this story represents about your true essence?

Authenticity

How often do you feel you embody the truest version of your-self in your day-to-day life? In which areas does this authentic expression come most easily? Hardest? Why do you think this is?

CREATING A SACRED SPACE

On your spiritual journey, it can be handy to have a sacred space where you can meditate, pray, use this journal, and commune with the spiritual world in whichever way you desire. It can be a favorite nook, chair, or corner—get creative!

1. Choose the space that you'd like to transform into your sacred space. Pick a space where you can see yourself feeling relaxed. Add a cushion, chair, or blanket to make it cozy and inviting.

2. Place some special objects in this area. Consider mementos, photos, crystals, or any items that inspire you.

3. Choose some mood lighting, such as a candle, a small light, or even a Himalayan salt lamp.

4. Lastly, add any final touches that help you get into a more reflective mood. These might include essential oils, incense, or a coaster for tea or energy-clearing herbs.

AFFIRMATION

I honor my divine essence by creating the time and space to connect to it.

Inspiration

Who is your spiritual role model? Are there mentors, teachers, authors, or public figures whom you resonate with? What about them speaks to you?

Values

Imagine you fast-forward far into the future and you're watching your own funeral. What are the things your friends and family are saying about you? What would you *want* people to remember you for?

Priorities

Our lives are made up of many facets, including family, career, health, love, friendships, and more. Which are your priorities right now? Are they reflected in how you spend your time? If not, what would need to change?

Clarity

Think about a decision in your life that makes you feel stuck.
Write down what you would do if you released any personal
or societal pressure, responsibility, financial factors, or other
barriers. What's the truth underneath it all?

Seasons of Life

Life has seasons that can reflect the ebb and flow of our personal journey. Our "summers" are full of social activities and opportunities. Personal "winters" are often quiet times of reflection and rest. Our "falls" are times of releasing and letting go, and when opportunity blossoms, we honor our "spring." What season are you in? How can you embrace its gifts?

Relationships

Our relationships are our greatest sources of growth. Reflect on the three to five people you spend the most time with. What lessons have you learned from each? Which of their qualities inspire you? How can they help you grow?

A CREATIVE PLAYDATE

We are born creators! When we tap into our creativity, we are connecting to our spiritual, or divine, essence. Today, create an inspiration board or book that will serve as a tool anytime you need help getting your creative juices flowing.

1. Choose a book with blank pages or some type of board for your canvas.

2. Decorate the pages or board. Attach words and pictures that inspire you, spark your creativity, or simply look beautiful. Think about images of your favorite places, people, landscapes, and beyond. You can use paint, markers, glitter—have fun with it.

3. Keep your creation somewhere that you will see it regularly and tap into it to rekindle your creative spark. If desired, continue working on it in future creative playdates!

AFFIRMATION

My creativity is an expression of my soul. I embrace my creative flow.

Happiness

More than any external factor, our happiness is dependent on the lens through which we look at the world. We all have negative things we could focus on, but today, list all the things you are choosing to be happy about!

Presence

What does it mean to you to live in the present moment? Share some examples of moments when you felt truly present and describe the factors that helped you be there.

Spirituality

What does spirituality mean to you? How does it show up in your life?

Awakening

What have been pivotal events on your awakening journey so far? How have each of them opened you up more spiritually? (Come back to this prompt every so often so you can reflect on the growing ways your journey has transformed you.)

Suffering

Do you believe that suffering is a natural part of the human condition? If so, what benefits might be gained from suffering? If not, what would life be like if we never experienced suffering? What has your experience of suffering taught you?

Vibration

If having a high vibration correlates with feelings and thoughts of love, positivity, and feeling spiritually connected, how would you describe your current vibration? What are some ways you could increase it?

A DAY WITH YOUR DESIRES

The desires and dreams we have in our heart are not random; they are unique expressions of our soul's calling and what we came here to experience and enjoy.

Spend an entire day tracking the desires that arise within you. What do you think about during the day? Do you daydream about starting a new job, spending more time doing something you love, or finding the romantic partner of your life? Do you fantasize about going on an exotic vacation? Log all your desires in a journal, smartphone, computer, or voice-recording tool. Review them before bed to bring more aware-ness to the direction your desires are taking you. Reflect on what you notice about your findings.

AFFIRMATION

My desires are divinely designed;
I can trust their wisdom.

Self-Worth

Where do you derive your self-worth from? Is it from your external circumstances or your spiritual connection? How is this working or not working for you?

Doubt

We all have self-doubt at times and in different areas of our life. Reflect on what would change in your life if you felt completely worthy of everything you desire. Would you take different actions, have different thoughts, or handle certain situations differently?

Growing Up and Out

Our core desire is to be loved, and as a child, we associated receiving love from our caregivers with survival. What characteristics did you develop to feel more lovable to them? Which ones benefit you today? Are there any that you are ready to let go of?

Self-Love

Reflect on the times when you have felt most in love with yourself. What were you doing? What do you think contributed to the self-love in that moment?

Relationships

What qualities are important to you in a romantic partner?
Which of these qualities do you possess yourself? What if
you became your own dream partner? What would this do
for your life?

_____

_____

_____

_____

_____

_____

_____

_____

_____

_____

_____

_____

_____

_____

_____

_____

_____

_____

_____

Self-Expression

Our soul, or spirit, wants to express itself in the physical! How do you enjoy expressing yourself? Do you feel that your appearance, home, career, or any other thing in your life reflects your full expression? If not, what would it look like if it did?

INNER PEACE POWER MOVE

Life throws situations at us that can tempt us to shift into anger, judgment, or frustration. How easy is it to disturb *your* peace? This simple meditation will help you ground back into your peace in minutes.

1. Close your eyes and take some deep breaths to relax your body.

2. As you breathe slowly, touch your thumbs to your pointer fingers and silently say, "Peace."

3. Breathing slowly, touch your thumbs to your middle fingers and silently say, "Begins."

4. Breathing slowly, touch your thumbs to your ring fingers and silently say, "With."

5. Breathing slowly, touch your thumbs to your pinky fingers and silently say, "Me."

Repeat for as long as needed. Even just a couple rounds of this meditation will shift you back into peace and remind you of your power. If you are unable to move in this way, you can simply combine the breaths with the words.

AFFIRMATION

My power is in my peace. I choose peace.

Self-Love

We spend so much time thinking about what we want to change about ourselves; however, we are all divinely designed. What are the qualities that you love most about yourself?

Surrender

Spiritual surrender allows us to relinquish control. It can mean inviting spirit into our lives so we can take action from a place of inspiration. Reflect on where in your life you've been controlling. How can you welcome more spiritual direction?

Heart Intelligence

Place your hand on your heart, connecting to the loving intelligence beating inside you. Fill up this whole page, starting each sentence with "My heart wants me to know . . ." Freewrite and allow the wisdom of your heart to flow.

Miracles

You are a living, breathing miracle, created from two cells combining. Allow yourself to ponder the miracle that is you and your physical body. Let it attune you to the very magic of your being. Jot down how this makes you feel.

Body Wisdom

Our body is always trying to communicate with us. It's an
instrument of our intuition. Take a few minutes to breathe,
notice your body, and connect with it; then freewrite any
messages that come up for you, starting with "My body wants
me to know . . ."

Mindful Eating

Reflect on your daily food choices. Do they fuel you and make you feel energized? Do you feel good about your choices? What would you change if you were mindful about what you put in your body?

MAKING A MANDALA

It is said that mandalas represent the journey of life and the path toward wisdom and self-realization. Drawing them helps bring us out of our thoughts and into a more meditative state.

1. Grab a piece of paper and pencil, plus colored pencils, markers, or something else to color with.

2. With the pencil, draw a small circle in the center of your paper. Draw bigger circles radiating out around the original.

3. Next, draw a line horizontally and vertically through the center. It should now look like a bull's-eye with a plus sign over it.

4. Starting from the smaller center pieces, draw the same pattern or shape, repeating in one wedge at a time. Fill each wedge with unique patterns and shapes, and color them in.

5. Feel free to put on some calming music, light a candle, and don't overthink. Just let your creativity flow!

AFFIRMATION

I relax my mind and allow it to flow freely.

Self-Care

Our habits, rituals, and daily self-care efforts set the stage for how we feel every day. What are five habits or activities that support you feeling your best? How can you make sure you do them regularly?

Intention

Everything is infused with the energy we bring to it. Therefore, setting intentions for each day or even for different activities can be transformational. What is your intention for the day or for your next activity? How will you bring this energy to the experience?

Compassion

Think of someone who is getting under your skin or irritating you in some way. Write down some possible scenarios that could be going on in their life that may be causing their behavior. Can you find compassion for them?

Self-Compassion

What's a quality about yourself that you often struggle with, and how can you reframe your perspective to be more compassionate toward yourself in this area?

Safety

Chakras are said to be the spiritual energy centers of the body. Your first energy center, or your root chakra, is said to be located at the base of your spine. It is your center for stability, security, and safety. What comes up for you around these themes? What activities help you tap into this chakra?

Creativity

Your second energy center, or your sacral chakra, is said to be located about six inches below your navel. It is your center for your creative and sexual energy. What comes up for you around its themes? How can you activate this energy?

A DAY OF SERVICE

Nothing can get us out of a funk better than being of service to someone else. When we put helping some-one else in front of whatever might be going on in our head, we shift into a more loving, spiritual energy. That means that when we are of service, we are also doing ourselves a great service!

Spend today looking for different ways to be of service, and log how you feel after your helpful act. It could be as simple as holding a door open for someone or running an errand for a friend. Try calling a friend or family member and ask them how they are doing. Get creative today and find three moments to be of service. Notice the magic!

AFFIRMATION

When I focus on service, I reconnect to my true spiritual self and feel better.

Personal Power

Your third energy center, or your solar plexus chakra, is said to be located at your navel center. It's your center for personal power, confidence, willpower, and responsibility. How's this center doing? How can you tap into it more?

Love

Your fourth energy center, or your heart chakra, is said to be located at your heart center. This center represents divine or unconditional love and self-love and governs relationships. Where's your heart chakra with its ruling themes? How can you tap into this center?

Communication

Your fifth energy center, or your throat chakra, is said to be located in the center of your throat. This center rules self-expression and truthfulness. How is your throat chakra doing based on these themes? How can you flex this energy center?

Intuition

Your sixth energy center, or your third-eye chakra, is said to be located slightly above the space between your eyebrows. It connects us to our intuition, imagination, and inner vision. How is your third-eye chakra doing? How can you use it more?

Higher Consciousness

Your seventh energy center, or your crown chakra, is located at the top of your head. It plugs into the spiritual and higher consciousness. How open and active do you feel your crown chakra is? How could you open yourself up to it more?

Gratitude

Gratitude is a powerful conduit of joy and an activator of our innate magnetic powers. Reflect on what you are most grateful for in your life today. Challenge yourself to think beyond the obvious!

TRANSCENDING DISCOMFORT

In this practice, we'll awaken our acceptance of a situation we may not be happy with and transcend its discomfort to discover what action we can take moving forward.

1. Close your eyes and focus on your breath for a few minutes. Begin to center yourself in the moment.

2. Visualize a situation that is causing disappointment or stress. Spend a few minutes here, sinking into the reality of this situation. Challenge yourself to sit in this discomfort and allow your breath to help you move gently but steadily through whatever feelings arise.

3. Continue until the feelings start to dissipate, hugging yourself or placing a hand on your heart to comfort yourself as necessary.

4. Ask yourself, "What's the next best step forward?" Focus on your breath until an answer naturally arises.

5. Trust what came through for you and follow its guidance.

AFFIRMATION

Acceptance of my present allows
me to choose my future.

Faith

Reflect on the concept of faith. What does having faith mean to you? How do you lean on your faith? In what ways can you increase your faith?

Spirituality

What is your relationship to your spiritual source? Write out what you believe to be true in your heart. The clearer you are about this relationship, the more connected you can feel spiritually.

Fate

Do you believe that certain events are fated? What if you adopted the belief that what's meant for you couldn't miss you— that if the job, lover, or opportunity was yours, it would always be yours? What would shift for you?

Expansion

Connecting to our own spiritual essence opens us up to our greater potential. What do you sense might shift in your life if you were more connected to this infinite space within you each day?

Frustration

Have you ever felt like the divine, your higher power or spiritual source, let you down? In a letter to that source, address any frustrations you may have had, and then immediately after, write a free-flowing letter responding to you from that same source. Trust whatever wants to come through!

Letting Go

Think of something in your life that you view as a problem. What thought does the problem originate from? Do you know that it's true? What would you (and your life) be like without this thought? Are you willing to let it go?

A RELEASING RITUAL

Just like we cleanse regularly, our energy field also likes to be cleaned out from the thoughts, patterns, and habits that no longer serve us. A powerful way to do this is with a releasing ritual.

1. On individual bits of scrap paper, write out thoughts, habits, or things in your life that you are ready to let go of.

2. Create a safe mini fire by lighting a candle in a glass jar.

3. One by one, take each paper into your hands. Close your eyes for a moment and tap into your spiritual essence. Read the paper out loud and feel the weight of this item on your soul. Open your eyes, carefully place the paper into the flame, and feel the weight lift as it turns to ash. Repeat for each item.

4. After your ritual, blow out your candle and savor the lightness.

AFFIRMATION

I release everything that
no longer serves me.

Higher Love

One of the most powerful spiritual practices is simply keeping an open heart. What ways do you close your heart throughout the day? How could you keep it open?

Spirituality

We all can pray, bless, or send good vibes to others. Our heart-centered energy uplifts us and all those we direct it at. Write a list of all the people in your life you want to send blessings to today—fill the whole page!

Peace

As we move further along our spiritual journey, peace often becomes more of a priority. Reflect on events, big and small, that have stolen your peace in the past, and write down creative ways to prevent them from shaking your calm in the future.

Forgiveness

Forgiveness is a sacred practice that brings us back home to the love and peace inside us. Withholding forgiveness hurts us more than it does the other person. Whom could you forgive today? Write a letter of forgiveness. (This note is just for your peace—no need to send it.)

Nature

Nature is a grand example of the divine design in everything. Reflect on nature's cycles, like the sunrise and sunset and leaves growing and dying. What feelings or thoughts did those or other observations bring up for you in your own life?

Emotions

Your spiritual awakening journey can bring up all sorts of feelings as you navigate this previously unknown territory. Reflect on the dominant emotions that have come up for you. How have they assisted in your growth? What have you learned about yourself?

CREATING A MEDICINE MANTRA

In the past, I've invited clients to come up with a "medicine mantra" to rewrite a persisting negative belief. It works wonders, so I'll share the simple process with you here.

1. Think of a persisting thought or belief that is negatively affecting your life. An example might be "There's something wrong with me."

2. Now flip it around. What would you like to believe instead? For the example in step 1, it could be "I am a divine (or spiritual) being, perfectly designed."

3. Meditate with your new medicine mantra. Set a timer for 20 minutes, close your eyes, and repeat your new mantra silently over and over again. Allow this empowering phrase to swirl around your body, enchant your mind, and hypnotize you into a peaceful haze. Repeat and use your medicine mantra as often as needed!

AFFIRMATION

I take back control of my thoughts and choose to design what is in my mind.

Consciousness

Do you believe you are your thoughts? What about your emotions? If not, who are you in relation to them? If so, how can you separate yourself from them?

Connection

When have you felt most connected to your spiritual side?
How could you incorporate this connectedness into your life to
regularly feel more "plugged in"?

Synchronicity

Synchronicities are moments of spiritual significance or, I like to say, "winks from the divine." Examples include seeing recurring numbers or being at the right place at the perfect time. Write down some synchronicities you've experienced and what they meant to you.

Intuition

Our intuition is the cosmic GPS we came into this world with so we would always be shown the path of our highest good. How does your intuition speak to you? How can you begin to listen to it more deeply and frequently?

Listening

Today, allow a message from your intuition to flow through. Ask yourself a question about something in your life, and then respond to it like you would to your best friend, letting the divine wisdom from inside you flow out on the page.

Joy

Our intuition speaks to us by naturally guiding us toward things that light us up. Rewrite your to-do list by prioritizing the tasks or activities that bring you the most joy.

TAPPING OUT FEAR AND DOUBT

Emotional freedom technique, also known as tapping, is a powerful therapeutic tool to help you release fear and doubt wherever you are.

1. Begin tapping the tips of your fingers on your right hand against the pinky side of your left hand.

2. As you tap, acknowledge your fear or doubt by saying, "Even though I feel [insert fear or doubt], I still love and accept myself." Repeat three times.

3. Acknowledge all the fears or doubts arising in your thought patterns.

4. Now as you tap, turn it around by saying, "Even though I feel these fears and doubts, I am willing to see them differently."

5. Implant the thoughts you want to believe. As you tap, declare: "I know the truth is that [insert the higher truth]." Repeat until you feel peace wash over you.

AFFIRMATION

I release my fears and doubts, and center back into my truth.

Appreciation

Gratitude and appreciation are the quickest ways we can raise our vibration (see page 20) and access a positive, uplifting mindset. Allow yourself to write everything that you can appreciate about your life, this day, and all the people in it!

Awareness

Take time today to reflect on what has shifted in your energy, outlook, and awareness since beginning this journal. Bringing this shift to your conscious awareness continues to expand it.

Highest Self

Our highest self is our most evolved self. It's the us that's following our heart's path and shining at its brightest. It's the greatest expression of our soul. Even if you may not have reached it yet, describe your highest self in all its glory!

Alignment

Life starts to really flow for us and feel good when we are in alignment with our higher selves. What actions, habits, or behaviors are out of alignment for you? What adjustments could you make to live in alignment with your higher self?

Expansion

Our spiritual path often takes us into the unknown, and it's where we grow the most! Reflect on areas in your life where you could lean on your faith and take a chance in the name of growth. What actions could you take?

Fears

Our fears often trip us up on the way to our desires. Think of the manifestation or reality you desire most in your life. What fears do you have around calling it in? For each fear, write what you would like to believe instead.

MOVING FOR A MIRACLE

In the groundbreaking metaphysical book *A Course in Miracles* by Helen Schucman, the miracle in discussion is a shift in perception from fear to love. Here, you'll bring to mind a situation that you want to see differently and, in doing so, open yourself up to receive the miracle of a higher perspective.

1. Find a peaceful place to go for a meditative stroll in whatever mode is comfortable for you.

2. As you do, consider a situation you're struggling with, and open yourself up to ask for divine help in seeing it differently.

3. Begin moving while holding your request in your heart.

4. Allow thoughts to arise naturally. Focus on your breath and stay present with what's in your heart as you move.

5. Allow your mind to naturally expand to see a higher, more loving perspective.

AFFIRMATION

I am ready for a miracle. I am willing to see this situation differently.

Unconscious Pain

If we associate any kind of pain with something we desire, we'll unconsciously stop ourselves from getting it. An example might be associating getting married with losing your friends. What possible painful scenarios can you associate with your desire? How can you navigate these scenarios to release what's blocking you?

Inner Child

Even small childhood occurrences can cause little traumas we carry into adulthood. Can you remember a time you didn't feel good enough as a child? What happened? What would you tell "little you" if you could go back and whisper into your younger self's ear?

Patterns

We often fall into patterns that can keep us stuck in a cycle until we consciously choose to do something differently. Think of an area of your life that's not working. Is there a pattern you see repeating there? How could you do things differently?

Transference

What facet of your life do you naturally excel at? Compare it with an area where you struggle. Now write down what's different about how you approach each area. Can you transfer some of the former characteristics to shift how you approach the latter?

Mindset

Our perspective changes our quality of life. We can look through a lens of "not enough" (time, money, opportunities, etc.) or abundance, possibilities, and potential. List areas you look at through a lens of lack. What would shift if you decided to see things through abundant eyes?

Decisions

If you knew that you could never make a wrong decision and that all paths would ultimately lead where you want to go, which areas of your life would feel easier? What decisions would you make?

PLUGGING INTO YOUR DIVINE LIGHT

This meditation will help you feel more connected, remind you who you truly are, and plug you back into your spiritual source, or divine light.

1. Close your eyes and breathe deeply, in through your nose and out your mouth. Bring your awareness to your heart center and imagine a golden ball of light glowing and growing with each breath.

2. Spend a few minutes watching that light expand until it covers your entire being.

3. Imagine a cord extending down from your heart center and wrapping itself around the core of the earth. Feel golden light rising from the earth and anchoring into your heart.

4. Now imagine divine light streaming down from above, through the crown of your head, plugging into your heart.

5. Breathe and receive these connections and feel yourself full of divine light. Spend as much time as you'd like here.

AFFIRMATION

I am plugged into the divine and anchored to the earth. I am full of light.

Thoughts, Part 1

Our mind can be either our biggest fan or our worst critic and can drastically affect our day. Fill this page with all the thoughts that regularly go through your head. Don't judge them; just observe them and write honestly.

Thoughts, Part 2

In the previous exercise, you brought your unconscious thoughts into your conscious awareness; this is the first step to shifting them. Today, fill the page with the thoughts you *want* to think for your highest good and happiness!

Mindfulness

What if every event in your life was inherently neutral and it was only your thoughts about those events that colored them either positive or negative? In what areas would you choose more positive thoughts? What would change because of this?

Mental Hygiene

News, social media, people in our life—everything we hear or see enters our mind and affects how we experience the world. What are you feeding your mind? Reflect on which sources lift you up and which bring you down. What do you *want* to be consciously feeding your mind?

Self-Sabotage

Our fears often manifest themselves in self-sabotaging behavior
that stops us from pursuing our dreams or being our highest
self. This might look like procrastination, emotional eating, or
something else. Reflect on your experience of this and how it's
evolving as you grow.

Releasing

As we grow, there are parts of ourselves, habits, thoughts, and relationships that no longer feel good for us. It's important to embrace the season of letting go. What are you ready to release? What's no longer serving you? How can you let it go with grace?

DIVINE REMINDERS

You've awakened to new truths about yourself on your spiritual journey, and now it's time to integrate these "divine truths" into your awareness. In this exercise, you'll explore some practical ways to give yourself divine reminders.

Choose which truths, medicine mantras (see page 63), or positive affirmations you'd like to remind yourself of, and pick any of the following items that resonate with you:

→ Set reminders on your phone for a divine reminder every hour or at mealtimes.

→ Post little love notes with your divine reminders in a place you'll see them often.

→ Set your screensaver to show a divine reminder or two.

→ Think of your own creative ways to incorporate reminders into your day!

AFFIRMATION

I reconnect to my divine truth daily.

Miracles

On page 77, we explored how miracles are a shift in perception from fear to love, making the impossible possible. What do you need a miracle around today? Write it out and ask your higher power to shift your mind from fear to love in this area.

Practical Action

What are three things in your life that you would like to make a positive change around or see something manifest from? For each area, brainstorm five practical actions you could take to move this energy forward.

Giving

Giving and receiving are two ends of the same branch. When we give, we also receive. Think about something you would really love to receive right now, and brainstorm ways you could *give* this very same thing to those around you.

Receiving

So many of us struggle with receiving. We deflect offers and gestures of help, compliments, and even the love of those around us. Use the following space to reflect on your relationship with receiving. Where could you allow yourself to receive more?

Angelic Guidance

Each of us has the ability to call on angels or other spiritual beings for divine support in our life; however, we need to actively ask them for their assistance. Write a letter to your spiritual guardian today. What can you ask for guidance on?

Reparenting

What are your favorite traits that you received from your parents or caregivers? How do these traits enhance your life? What are your least favorite traits from your parents or caregivers? How can you navigate them in a way that's more beneficial?

ENERGETIC HOUSE CLEANING

Now that you're raising your vibration (see page 20) and learning more about who you truly are, certain items in your personal spaces may no longer resonate with you. Your energy is simply no longer aligned to these old items, making it a good time to release them.

Take a couple hours to do a sweep of your personal spaces and gather the items that don't feel good to you anymore or simply don't belong now. Trust your intuition on this and know that each object you release creates space for more beautiful things that are in alignment with your next-level you.

Consider donating, gifting, or selling these items so they can be helpful to those who may need them.

AFFIRMATION

I release all that no longer serves me to create space for what is on its way.

Purpose

Is there a hardship that you've overcome that you could help someone else through? Is there a lesson you've learned that you'd like to pass on? If you could share a message via a speech, book, letter, or billboard, what would it be?

Oneness

The core of the spiritual journey is realizing that we are all one; we are all divinely connected. How have you experienced this concept? In what ways do you feel more connected to all beings?

Community

Describe your vision for the world. What would change?
What kind of world would you love to be a part of creating?

Past Lives

Do you believe your soul lived other lifetimes? If not, use the following questions as a creative exercise or to address any sense of déjà vu. Are there certain historical periods or places that you feel a strong connection to? If you were to guess a prior incarnation of yours, what would it be? Is there anything from that incarnation you can draw upon to assist you today?

Soul Growth

Some believe that when we incarnate, we choose the lessons, environment, and core relationships for this life. If this is true, why do you think you chose your situation? What kind of learning journey might have appealed to your soul?

Impact

We are the eyes, ears, hands, and feet of divine substance here on earth, and because of that, each of us is called to serve in different ways. What problems in the world tug most on your heartstrings? How could you make an impact in these areas?

CONNECTING TO THE INFINITE OCEAN

We are all connected to infinity at our deepest essence. This meditation will help you experience more of the infinite ocean of your soul.

1. Close your eyes and start focusing on your breath. Breathe deeply, in through your nose and out your mouth. Allow any thoughts that arise to float on by, focusing on your breath.

2. Bring your awareness to your navel center. As you breathe, envision yourself diving into endless space through your navel center. Continue this dive for a few minutes.

3. Imagine yourself on the other side of your navel center, floating in an infinite ocean. Feel the warmth, love, and safety of this ocean all around you. Continue to breathe and enjoy the feeling of floating in an endless sea for several more minutes, soaking up this connection to your own infinity.

AFFIRMATION

I am a drop in an infinite ocean.
My very essence is endless.

Divine Support, Part 1

What if I told you that you had a divine support squad? This squad could consist of any entity—angels, spirit guides, loved ones who have passed on, or whatever or whomever speaks to you. Who would be on your squad? How would it feel to know you have this support?

Divine Support, Part 2

Consider that your divine support squad is there for guidance and support at all times if you want them to be. Let's start a habit of communicating with them. Write a letter asking them for what you would like their help with in your life right now.

Spirit World

Have you ever connected with a spirit or a loved one who passed on? If so, write about your experience and what you believe about the spirit world. If not, do you believe it's possible? Would you be open to receiving signs or having such an experience?

Spiritual Truth

Reflect on what you feel is the highest truth about yourself.
Who are you? What is your spiritual, or divine, truth?

Channeling

It's time to allow your divine truth to flow through you. Start freewriting, beginning each sentence with "The divine truth is . . ." and allow whatever comes forward to fill up the page.

Spirituality

Reflect on the spiritual, or divine, truth that has brought you the most peace and/or understanding. If you could pass only one truth on to the rest of the world and future generations, what would it be and why?

Reflection

The spiritual awakening journey leads us to living in the world in a way that is not of this world. We look at the world through new eyes, seeing new truth. Reflect on what this means to you.

Perspective

How has your life changed since embarking on your spiritual path? What blessings have since come into your life? How have your relationships changed? How has your perspective changed? Describe all the ways life has shifted.

Potential

A positive side effect of having a stronger spiritual connection is the ability to tap into more of your own divine potential. What new possibilities have opened up for you? What are you going to take action on going forward?

Growth

The spiritual awakening journey is about choosing love, growth, and possibilities in a world that tries to tempt us into fear and limitation. How will you keep this power moving forward? What tools or practices will you use? What truths will you keep close?

Resources

Books

Eat with Intention: Recipes and Meditations for a Life That Lights You Up by Cassandra Bodzak
Is part of your spiritual awakening journey connected to your body and/or self-love? You'll love the meditations, wisdom, and soul-nourishing recipes in my first book.

Manifesting Through Meditation: 100 Guided Practices to Harness the Power of Your Thoughts and Create the Life You Want by Cassandra Bodzak
An important part of your spiritual awakening journey is having a daily meditation practice. In my second book, you will find a variety of ways to explore meditation, how to use meditation to improve your life, and how to settle into a powerful daily mindfulness ritual.

Neville Goddard: The Complete Reader
This collection of works by American mystic Neville Goddard is one of the most powerful texts on manifestation and metaphysics. If you want to learn more as you make your way deeper into your spiritual journey, these classic texts will be invaluable.

The Power of Now by Eckhart Tolle
The ultimate book on how to live in the present moment, it's incredible for navigating difficult times and an essential part of your spiritual awakening library.

A Return to Love by Marianne Williamson
For those curious about the metaphysical text *A Course in Miracles*, Marianne Williamson's book breaks down its essential wisdom in a way that is accessible, delightful, and life-changing. This book is a powerful guide to looking at the world through new eyes.

The Seat of the Soul by Gary Zukav
In this classic, Gary Zukav demystifies the journey back to our soul or spirit as well as the collective spiritual awakening process. It's one of the essential books I find myself recommending over and over to clients.

The Untethered Soul by Michael A. Singer
When I hear someone is beginning their spiritual awakening journey, this is my first book recommendation. Michael A. Singer brilliantly breaks down mindfulness in a way that creates so many "ahas" about who you are and how to separate yourself from your thoughts.

Online

Clarity, Miracles, and Momentum Virtual Retreat
CassandraBodzak.Teachable.com/p/clarity-miracles-and
-momentum-virtual-retreat
Want to take a weekend at home to go deep, get clear on your vision, and do some powerful work to clear the fears that are blocking you from believing you are cocreating with the divine? Check out this on-demand virtual retreat for a game-changing weekend.

Divine Downloads
CassandraBodzak.com/cat/the-podcast
If you loved exploring the spiritual concepts in this journal, you'll really enjoy the interviews and deep-dive solo-casts on the podcast. Use it as a way to continue going deeper and staying inspired on your spiritual awakening journey.

Divinely Design Your Life
www.DivinelyDesignYourLife.com
My own personal resource, this site includes a free guided
meditation bundle, a free virtual manifesting workshop, and my
signature spiritual group-coaching program, which includes
teachings, meditations community, and biweekly live calls to
support you in making the vision for your life your reality.

The Unplug Meditation App
Unplug.com/online-classes
This app is great if you're looking for more guided meditations
to help you get into the groove of a daily practice. I have several
meditations on the Unplug app, available in all app stores, that
can help you get started.

Follow Me on Social Media
I put out tons of free content through my social media and
YouTube channel each week—everything from live talks to guided
meditations and tools for divinely designing your life.

CassandraBodzak.com

Clubhouse: @cassandrabodzak

Facebook.com/cassandrabodzak

Instagram.com/cassandrabodzak

TikTok.com/@cassandrabodzak

YouTube.com/cassandrabodzakTV

Acknowledgments

Thank you to my wonderful fiancé for always holding space for my writing and creative ventures. Thank you to my mother for instilling a love of journaling in me from a young age and my father for encouraging all my entrepreneurial endeavors. Thank you to my incredible stepdaughter for the inspiration to leave even more tools behind to guide others along this most magical journey. Thank you to all the wonderful women who have worked with me over the years, who have given me the divine pleasure of guiding them along this spiritual journey. Big, huge thank-you to Eun H. Jeong for being an amazing editor and helping me make this journal the best it could be!

About the Author

 **Cassandra Bodzak** is a thought leader, best-selling author, and sought-after on-camera personality and speaker in the mindfulness and personal development world. She is the host of the popular spiritual podcast *Divine Downloads*. You may have seen Cassandra on ABC's *The Taste* with Anthony Bourdain as the "happy, healthy-living guru" or in her work with *Shape*, *EatingWell*, HuffPost, Teen Vogue, *Thrive*, Fabletics, Lululemon, SoulCycle, and many more media outlets. She has been called "an award-winning thought leader and intuitive coach" in *Forbes* and "a spiritual leader" by Well+Good. Cassandra helps people all over the world learn the process for bringing their soul's desires into their everyday reality through her online group program, Divinely Design Your Life, as well as through all the free content she shares on her YouTube channel and other social media.

CPSIA information can be obtained
at www.ICGtesting.com
Printed in the USA
JSHW010920310322
24484JS00009B/23

9 781638 077992